HOLT

U.S. Supreme Court
Case Studies

HOLT, RINEHART AND WINSTON
A Harcourt Education Company

Orlando • **Austin** • New York • San Diego • Toronto • London

Written by the American Bar Association Division for Public Education:
Standing Committee Chair Alan Kopit; Division Director Mabel McKinney-Browning;
Contributing Writers Charles White, Charles Williams, and Katie Fraser; Contributing Editor
Michelle Parrini.

The views expressed in this publication are those of the authors and have not been approved
by the House of Delegates or the Board of Governors of the American Bar Association
and, accordingly, should not be construed as representing the policy of the American Bar
Association or the Fund for Justice and Education.

ISBN 0-03-041924-7

3 4 5 6 7 082 08 07 06

Contents

The Supreme Court in American Life

The U. S. government has three branches. Two of them are very well known. These are the legislative branch (Congress) and the executive branch (the President and federal agencies).

The third branch, the judicial branch, is a little mysterious to most people. The judicial branch is composed of the federal courts. It is a separate branch of government, created by Article III of the Constitution. The role of the courts is to decide legal cases. In doing that, courts apply the laws and the Constitution. They have to interpret these laws—that is, decide exactly what the language of law means. Courts also have to decide whether these laws are consistent with the Constitution. If they are not, the courts will declare that the laws are unconstitutional and strike such laws down. That is, the courts will declare that all or a portion of these laws are void—as if they had never existed.

This power to decide the constitutionality of a law is called judicial review. It is the courts' greatest power. Because of their ability to declare laws of Congress and actions of the President unconstitutional, the courts have a place as a co-equal branch of government.

The United States Supreme Court is at the head of the federal court system. It is our nation's highest court. The Supreme Court has the authority to hear appeals from the lower federal courts. If necessary, it can reverse their rulings. The Court also has the power in certain circumstances to hear cases that began in the state courts. The Supreme Court can reverse the rulings of state courts and even state supreme courts that conflict with the Constitution. The United States Supreme Court is truly the most important court in the country.

The judges on the Supreme Court are called justices. The Supreme Court is composed of nine justices—a Chief Justice and eight associate justices. Congress has the power to pass laws that determine the number of justices. Congress has changed this number several times throughout American history. There were originally six justices on the Court. The number has been set at nine since 1869.

The President nominates the Chief Justice and the other justices. The Senate must confirm them (agree that they should become justices) before they can begin to serve. Thus the legislative and executive branches have control over who becomes a justice. However, once the nominations are confirmed and the justices named to the Court, the Constitution tries to assure that they are independent of the other two branches. The Constitution gives Supreme Court justices (and other federal judges) life tenure. That means they can serve until death, or until they choose to retire. They can only be removed from office by impeachment, after they are convicted of committing certain crimes. In all of American history no Supreme Court justice has ever been removed from office by impeachment. Moreover, the salaries of the justices and other federal judges can't be reduced while they are in office. This means that Congress can't punish them for making unpopular decisions by reducing their pay.

The Constitution gives the Supreme Court the authority to hear certain kinds of cases. If the Court has jurisdiction (authority to hear a case), the parties that have lost their case in a lower court can file a request for a Supreme Court hearing. If the Court agrees to hear their case, the parties have the chance to get that loss overturned. If the Court turns the parties down, their case is very probably over. The decision of the lower court will stand.

The Supreme Court does not have to hear every case it is asked to hear. In fact, the Court chooses to hear very few cases. In recent decades it has heard only about 80 to 90 cases a year, which it selects from about 7,000 requests. These are typically the cases that the Court believes raise the most important issues.

How Does the Court Decide a Case?

When the Court agrees to hear a case, it asks the lawyers for the parties (the people or organizations involved) to file written arguments. These arguments are printed in booklets that are limited to 50 pages. In these documents (called briefs) the lawyers say why the law or the Constitution supports their position. People and groups who are not involved in the case but have an interest in the outcome can also file briefs. These people are called amici curiae (Latin for "friends of the court"). Their briefs are called amicus briefs.

After reading the parties' briefs, the Court hears their oral arguments. Each side is usually given 30 minutes to explain why the law supports their position. The justices often ask the lawyers questions to clarify their arguments. They also often ask the lawyers to explain how a decision one way or the other would affect other cases that might arise in the future.

The Supreme Court does not permit the attorneys to introduce evidence or produce witnesses at oral argument. This is because the Court does not set out to decide "the facts" in any case before it. Instead, the justices typically accept as true the fact findings made by the lower courts. This frees the Court to review just the legal questions in the case.

In the weeks (and sometimes months) after oral argument, the justices meet to discuss the case. These meetings are private. The justices share their views on the case, discuss the law that applies to the case, and eventually vote on how the case should be decided.

If the decision is unanimous (that is, if every justice agrees), the Chief Justice will either write the opinion or appoint one of the other justices to write it. The opinion gives the decision of the Court and the reasoning behind the decision. If the decision is not unanimous, the majority opinion will give the decision and the reasoning. One or more of the justices who did not agree (the dissenters) will write an opinion discussing how they think the case should have been decided. This is called a dissenting opinion.

There is a third type of opinion. It is the concurring opinion. It is written by a justice who agrees (concurs) with the majority's decision to affirm or reverse the lower court, but not with the majority's reasons for doing so. Such a justice may write a "concurring" opinion explaining the justice's view of the case.

The Court and the Other Branches

Is the Court a weak branch or a strong branch? Those who think it is a weak branch could point out that the justices are not elected, so that they can't claim to speak for the people. They can't issue opinions on issues whenever they want. They can only decide actual legal cases that they have been asked to hear. That means they don't have complete control over their "docket." Even if the justices all agree on a point, they can't express it until it comes up in a case that they have been asked to decide.

One of the Founders, Alexander Hamilton, pointed out another reason why the Court might not be viewed as powerful. In the Federalist Papers (#78), he wrote that the judicial branch is "the weakest of the three departments of power." Hamilton said that the judiciary controlled neither the budget nor the military. The judiciary "may truly be said to have neither FORCE nor WILL, but merely judgment; and must ultimately depend upon the aid of the executive arm even [to carry out] its judgments." Sometimes Presidents have been reluctant to enforce the Court's orders. President Andrew Jackson is supposed to have said after one decision he did not like, "[Chief Justice] John Marshall has made his decision. Let him enforce it."

Perhaps in recognition of this weakness, until 1935 the Court did not have its own building. Congress has the Capitol. The President has the White House. For most of its history, the Court had just a few rooms in the Capitol, with Congress getting most of the space.

Supreme Court Cases

But the Court in many ways is a very powerful branch of government. "It is very quiet here," said Justice Oliver Wendell Holmes, "but it is the quiet at the eye of the storm." Though the Court does not speak on every issue, in the cases it decides, it has the final word. Congress may pass a bill. The President may sign it into law. But if the Court says it is unconstitutional, it is as if the law never existed. And the justices can't be voted out of office. They can't be fired.

The justices draw their strength from the Constitution. They have the final authority to determine what it means and how it applies. Yes, Congress can try to pass a new law to get around a problem the Court found in an earlier law. However, that new law itself may come before the Court and be struck down. Yes, the Constitution can be amended, but that has happened only a few times in more than 200 years.

Periods When the Court Has Been Powerful

The strength of the Court depends on its members, and especially on its Chief Justices. John Marshall was the Court's first great Chief Justice. He served on the Court for almost 35 years, but his greatness had more to do with his leadership than with the length of time he served.

John Adams, who had been defeated for re-election, appointed Marshall Chief Justice in early 1801, just before he left office. The political party of Adams and Marshall, the Federalists, never again held power. In fact, the party no longer existed in the last 20 years that Marshall was on the Court. That means that Marshall had to lead justices who had been named by presidents who were not sympathetic to Marshall's political beliefs. Nonetheless, he did lead them, brilliantly. Most of the great decisions of the Marshall Court were unanimous, and were written by Marshall himself.

These decisions

- established the Court's power to declare laws unconstitutional (judicial review)

- established the Court's right to review and reverse state court decisions in certain circumstances

- interpreted the Constitution broadly, to give the federal government powers over interstate commerce and more authority in conflicts with the states

Though he did not help write the Constitution, Chief Justice John Marshall is rightly considered one of the Founders. More than anyone, he is responsible for establishing the authority of the Supreme Court as equal with the legislative and executive branches.

Probably the Court made the most impact on American life under Chief Justice Earl Warren. Warren came from California. He was governor of that state in 1953, when President Eisenhower nominated him to be Chief Justice. Warren retired from the Court in 1969. He served only half as long as Marshall, yet under his leadership the Court handed down many decisions that reshaped American law and American life. Of the 25 key cases we cover in this book, the Warren Court decided several, including

- *Brown* v. *Board of Education*, which struck down school segregation

- *Baker* v. *Carr*, which paved the way for major changes in Congressional and legislative districts

- *Engel* v. *Vitale*, which struck down organized prayer in the schools

- *Miranda* v. *Arizona*, one of a long series of decisions that reshaped criminal law

- *Tinker* v. *Des Moines*, a landmark case that established the constitutional rights of students

The Warren Court used the Equal Protection Clause and the Due Process Clause of the 14th Amendment to strike down many, many state laws. These broad decisions greatly affected schools, the police, politics, race relations, and other areas that touched the lives of all Americans.

Supreme Court Cases

The Warren Court's decisions were controversial at the time. Many, such as the school prayer decision, are still controversial. Critics of the Warren Court charge that it went too far. They say that the Court should have left many of these matters to local authorities to decide. They say that many of the problems addressed by the Court in these cases could have been better taken care of through the political process, by new laws passed by the legislature. Warren's defenders point out that the Constitution is the supreme law of the land. The decisions of the Warren Court, they say, upheld the Constitution and moved our nation closer to its great ideals of justice and equality.

Conclusion

Though the Court is making fewer landmark decisions today than it was under Earl Warren, it has decided some very important cases. Examples include its decision forcing President Nixon to hand over tapes that led to his impeachment and the 2000 case of *Bush* v. *Gore,* in which the Court's decision determined who would be President.

The balance between the branches is not static. We can't predict how the relationship of the branches will play out in the future. But one thing is certain. The U.S. Supreme Court will continue to influence the course of American history and the lives of Americans.

How to Use This Book

The core of this book is 25 of the most important Supreme Court cases. Each is discussed in two pages. Questions and activities follow each case. In our discussion of many cases, we refer you to other important cases that you will find online. Simply access www.abanet.org/publiced/resources for brief discussions of these cases.

If you want to explore cases further, you can find them online in many sites. For brief summaries of a case and the full decision, access http://supct.law.cornell.edu/supct/ or http://www.findlaw.com/casecode/supreme.html. To use these sites you just need to put in one of the names in the case (for example, "Lochner" for *Lochner* v. *New York*). Or you can put in the case citation. This simply tells you where you might find a case in a book that collects the Court's decisions. For example, the citation for *Lochner* is 198 U.S. 45 (1905). We give you the full citation of each case in this book's table of contents.

Case 1: Marbury v. Madison (1803)   Judicial Review

 THE ISSUE Who should decide whether a law is constitutional?

WHAT'S AT STAKE?

Whether the U.S. Supreme Court can strike down laws that are not consistent with the Constitution.

FACTS AND BACKGROUND

In 1800, Thomas Jefferson won the presidential election. President John Adams lost. Before Jefferson was inaugurated, Adams nominated 42 of his supporters as justices of the peace for the District of Columbia.

The new justices of the peace could not take office until they received a signed and sealed document called a *commission*. John Marshall, the acting secretary of state, did not have time to deliver all of the commissions. Soon after Jefferson took office, he found that some of the commissions had not been delivered. He ordered James Madison, the new secretary of state, not to deliver them.

William Marbury was one of the people who did not receive his commission. Marbury asked the Supreme Court for a special order, called a *writ of mandamus*, to force Madison to deliver the commission. The Constitution lists the types of cases that the Supreme Court can hear. The list does not include cases where a person is seeking mandamus. But the Judiciary Act (1789) said that people could go directly to the Supreme Court to seek this kind of order. *Marbury* v. *Madison* began in the Supreme Court.

The Chief Justice of the Supreme Court was John Marshall, the same man who had failed to deliver Marbury's commission. Marshall was a political opponent of Jefferson. Marshall and the Court faced a difficult decision. If the Court ordered Madison to deliver Marbury's commission, Jefferson and Madison would likely ignore the order. The Court would look weak. If the Court denied Marbury's claim, it would look like it was backing down to the President.

THE DECISION

The vote on the Court was unanimous. Chief Justice Marshall wrote the Court's opinion. He said that Marbury had a legal right to receive his commission. Furthermore, Madison's refusal to deliver it violated that right. But then Marshall did something surprising.

Marshall wrote that the Judiciary Act conflicted with the U.S. Constitution. The Constitution listed the types of cases the Supreme Court could hear. The Judiciary Act added to that list. When two laws conflict, Marshall wrote, the courts must decide which law to follow. The Constitution is the supreme law of the land. As a result, the Court declared that the Judiciary Act was unconstitutional.

In his decision, Chief Justice Marshall gave up the Court's power to hear the types of cases listed in the Judiciary Act. Instead, Marshall claimed a far greater right for the Court—the power of judicial review. He wrote,

> *It is emphatically* [definitely] *the province* [role] *and duty of the judicial department to say what the law is… If two laws conflict with each other, the courts must decide on the operation of each.*

IMPACT OF THE DECISION

Judicial review means that the judiciary is able to check the power of Congress and the President. Judicial review makes the Supreme Court one of the three great branches of government. This power is essential to the checks and balances of our system. It has been used often in the past 200 years.

QUESTIONS

1. Without the power of judicial review, who would decide whether laws were constitutional? What problems might arise if the same branch of government both passed laws and decided if they were constitutional?

_____

_____

2. Do you think that nine judges should be able to decide whether laws created by an elected body are unconstitutional? Explain your answer.

_____

_____

FIND OUT

What types of cases can the Supreme Court hear?

Case 2: McCulloch v. Maryland (1819)

Federalism

> **THE ISSUES** Does the Constitution give Congress the power to establish a national bank? If so, does the Constitution allow Maryland to tax that bank?

FACTS AND BACKGROUND

Congress set up the Bank of the United States in 1816. The states opposed it because their own state banks were losing business to it. Several states placed heavy taxes on branches of the national bank. These national bank branches refused to pay those taxes.

For example, in Maryland, the branch of the national bank refused to pay Maryland state taxes. The Maryland state government sued the bank's cashier, James McCulloch. In 1819, the case reached the Supreme Court.

THE DECISION

Every Justice on the Court agreed that the Constitution *did* allow Congress to establish a national bank. They also agreed that it did *not* allow Maryland to tax the bank.

Writing for the Court, Chief Justice Marshall pointed out "The government proceeds directly from the people…. Its powers are granted by them, and are to be exercised [used]… for their benefit." Thus the U. S. Constitution is superior to ordinary laws, including laws passed by the states. If a state law conflicts with the Constitution, it cannot be valid.

Implied Powers Article I, Section 8, of the Constitution lists the powers of Congress. It does not include or exclude the power to charter a bank. It also states that Congress may make all laws that are "necessary and proper" for carrying out the listed powers. Marshall said that many important powers are listed in the Constitution, and the rest can be "deduced" [implied] as necessary to carry out the listed powers. Certainly, a national bank helps the government carry out such listed powers as collecting taxes, borrowing money, and supporting armies and navies. Therefore, the Constitution permits it.

Federal Supremacy Marshall said that if the states could tax one of the federal government's activities, they could tax any of them. But "the power to tax involves the power to destroy." The states could try to tax the mail, the federal courts, and the army. This could not be permitted because of the wording in the second paragraph of Article VI. According to this "supremacy clause," the Constitution and laws of the federal government are the "supreme law of the land." *Supremacy* means being of the highest authority or rank. A *clause* is a specific section in a document. The Constitution binds judges in every state, even if state law conflicts with the Constitution. If a state law conflicts with the Constitution, that law cannot be valid.

WHY THE CASE IS IMPORTANT

This case contains two important principles.

The principle of implied powers The Court greatly expanded what the Constitution allows the federal government to do. Today, Congress has many "implied powers" that allow it to make laws that are "necessary and proper" to carry out its listed powers.

The principle of national supremacy The federal Constitution and federal laws come before the constitutions and laws of the states. When the federal government is using powers that belong to it, the states must give way.

QUESTIONS

1. Where in the Constitution can you find the principle of implied powers? The principle of national supremacy?

_____

_____

2. What are the advantages to Marshall's "broad" interpretation of the Constitution? What are its disadvantages?

_____

_____

FIND OUT

In 1819, many people believed that the Constitution should be interpreted narrowly. They believed Congress had no implied powers. Others believed the Constitution should be interpreted broadly to give Congress implied powers. Can you find other examples of this debate in our history?

ONLINE EXTRA

Daniel Webster was the winning lawyer in *McCulloch* v. *Maryland*. He argued an astonishing 249 cases before the Court, including the Dartmouth College case (see online discussion).

Case 3: Gibbons v. Ogden (1824)

Federalism

THE ISSUE What is the proper balance between the states and the federal government under the Constitution's Commerce Clause?

FACTS AND BACKGROUND

In 1824, New York law said that no one could operate a steamboat on any of the state's waterways without first getting a state license. Aaron Ogden had such a New York license. It gave him a monopoly [exclusive control] on using New York waters. Nevertheless, Thomas Gibbons began operating a ferry between Manhattan and New Jersey. Gibbons didn't have a New York license, but he did have a federal "coasting" license. Ogden sued to stop Gibbons from operating his boats in New York waters. The state courts upheld Ogden's monopoly on running steamboats in New York.

Gibbons appealed to the U.S. Supreme Court. He argued that the New York law was *void* [not valid] under the Commerce Clause of the Constitution.

The Commerce Clause (Art. I, Sect. 8) says that Congress has the power "To regulate Commerce with foreign Nations, and among the several States, and with the Indian Tribes." In *Gibbons* v. *Ogden* the Court had to interpret its meaning.

The first question was did "commerce" only include buying and selling goods, or did it cover things like operating passenger ships? Secondly, if the Commerce Clause gave Congress the power to regulate passenger ships between states, could the states still enforce their own laws in this area?

THE DECISION

Chief Justice Marshall wrote the opinion of the Court. His opinion struck down the New York law under the Commerce Clause. Marshall wrote that in drafting a Constitution, the Framers wanted to rescue commerce from "embarrassing and destructive consequences, resulting from the legislation of so many different States, and to place it under the protection of a uniform law."

Marshall pointed out the problems posed by the overlapping and conflicting state laws in this case. Under New York law, no one could navigate any of the state's waters by steamboat *without* a New York license. But under the law of Connecticut, no one could enter Connecticut waters with a steam vessel that *had* such a New York

U.S. Supreme Court Case Studies

license. Marshall's opinion held that the Commerce Clause prevents states from enforcing such conflicting laws.

What is "Commerce"?

Marshall reasoned that commerce was more than buying and selling goods. "The mind can scarcely conceive a system for regulating commerce … which shall exclude all laws concerning navigation." Thus, under the Commerce Clause, Gibbons' federal license rendered the New York monopoly void.

What Role Do the States Have?

This important question was left undecided by Marshall's opinion. For example, would such a state law as New York's have been valid if there had *not* been a conflicting federal license? When there is no federal law, can a state write laws to fill the void?

Marshall was sympathetic to the view that the Commerce Clause gave Congress sole power to regulate commerce between the states. Under this interpretation, while the Clause does not authorize Congress to regulate purely *intrastate* commerce (that is, commerce taking place wholly within one state's borders), only Congress can regulate commerce between the states. Today, Congress does regulate commerce between the states, while each state regulates commerce within its own borders.

QUESTION

1. How did this decision strengthen the power of the federal government and weaken the power of the states?

    _____

    _____

FIND OUT

1. What was commerce between the states like under the Articles of Confederation? What problems occured?

2. Read the New Deal cases in this book. What was the debate over the Commerce Clause during the New Deal of the 1930s? How did it turn out?

Case 4: Worcester v. Georgia (1832)

Indian Nations

 THE ISSUE Can Georgia enforce its criminal laws inside the boundaries of the Cherokee Nation?

WHAT'S AT STAKE?

For a state, whether it could ignore federal laws and treaties and assert its own authority over territory that had been awarded to an Indian tribe. For Indian tribes, whether they had authority over their territory, could govern themselves, and enforce their own laws.

FACTS AND BACKGROUND

Under a treaty, the federal government recognized the right of the Cherokee Nation to their land in Georgia. Congress also gave the Cherokees certain rights to govern themselves. By 1828, Georgia wanted authority over the Cherokees in the state. Over the next several years, Georgia passed laws to abolish or replace tribal laws.

Georgia's policy led to two Supreme Court cases known as "the Cherokee Cases." The first case was *Cherokee Nation* v. *Georgia* (1831). In it, the Cherokees asked the Court to issue an injunction, which is a court order that usually stops an action from taking place. The Cherokees wanted to keep the state from interfering with the tribe's self-governance. Because the Cherokees as a tribe were asking the Court to hear the case, they had to show that they were an independent foreign state. The Court rejected that description. Instead, Chief Justice Marshall wrote, the Cherokee Nation was a "domestic dependent nation." He said their relationship to the United States resembles that of a "ward to his guardian." The Court declined to rule on the injunction. It reasoned it did not have the authority because the tribe wasn't a foreign nation.

This ruling was fatal to the tribe's suit. However, some aspects of the Court's opinion supported the Cherokees. For one, the Chief Justice wrote that the justices accepted the tribe's argument that it was "a state . . . a distinct political society, separated from others, capable of managing its own affairs and governing itself."

The stage was set for *Worcester* v. *Georgia* the following year. Two missionaries had been sentenced to four years "hard labor" in the state prison. Their crime: violating a new Georgia law that prohibited any "white person" from living in Cherokee territory without first getting a state license and taking an oath to support the laws of Georgia. The missionaries appealed their case to the Supreme Court.

U.S. Supreme Court Case Studies

Case 4: Worcester v. Georgia, *continued*   Indian Nations

THE DECISION

The Supreme Court reversed the missionaries' convictions. Chief Justice Marshall said all Congressional laws and treaties giving the Cherokees their rights "manifestly consider the several Indian nations as distinct political communities, having territorial boundaries, within which their authority is exclusive." Marshall said that Georgia laws had no force in Cherokee Nation territory.

THE IMPACT OF THE DECISION

Because of this decision, states must respect tribal sovereignty. Today, Indian nations have much more sovereignty than cities or counties, though less than foreign nations. Historically, the case is best known for its tragic aftermath. The missionaries remained in jail until eventually "pardoned" by the governor. More importantly, President Andrew Jackson refused to enforce it. He was determined to seize tribal territory east of the Mississippi River.

The federal government eventually persuaded about 500 of the 17,000 Cherokee in Georgia to agree to a new treaty. On the basis of this treaty, the entire Cherokee Nation, including the women, children, and the elderly, were forced at gunpoint to march 1,000 miles in the winter of 1838–1839. They went to so-called "Indian Territory" west of the Mississippi. Some 4,000 Cherokee died along this trail, known in Cherokee as "The Trail Where They Cried" and in English as "The Trail of Tears."

QUESTIONS

1. If an Indian reservation lies within a state's boundaries, why can't a state simply enforce its laws on the reservation just like it can anywhere else in the state?

_____

_____

2. How can a state be forced to follow a Supreme Court decision with which it disagrees?

_____

_____

ONLINE EXTRA

Read the online case of *United States* v. *Lara*. What did this case say about the authority of an Indian tribe to enforce its own laws? How is this similar to what the Court said in *Worcester* v. *Georgia*?

Case 5: Dred Scott v. Sandford (1857)

Rights of African Americans

 THE ISSUES Does the Constitution give an African American the right to sue in federal court? Does the Constitution allow Congress to make a law that takes slaves away from people who bring them into a free territory?

WHAT'S AT STAKE

The case was important for all Americans. In 1857, the country was bitterly divided over slavery. Many historians think the Court tried to resolve the slavery question by deciding this case.

FACTS AND BACKGROUND

In 1833, John Emerson purchased a slave named Dred Scott. Emerson later took Scott to the Wisconsin Territory. Slavery was illegal in Wisconsin Territory under the Missouri Compromise (1820). Scott believed that because he had lived for years on free soil, he should be free.

In 1848, the United States won the war against Mexico. The boundaries of the nation now stretched clear to California. Clearly, the issue of slavery in new territories had to be settled. In 1852, after six years in the courts, the Supreme Court of Missouri ruled against Scott. By 1856, Scott's case finally went to the Supreme Court. Because the issues it raised were so important, the Court asked the parties to argue the case twice. In *Brown* v. *Board of Education* (1954), another key case about race in America, the Court also requested two arguments.

THE DECISION

The Court ruled that African Americans could not sue in federal court. It also ruled that Congress did not have the power to make a law taking slaves away from people who bring them into a free territory.

Race and citizenship Chief Justice Roger Taney wrote the decision for the majority of seven justices. Two other justices *dissented* [disagreed]. Taney's opinion reflected the prejudices of the day. He said that African Americans had "none of the rights and privileges" of citizens. This statement applied not only to slaves, but also to free blacks.

The chief justice ignored an important fact. In many states, blacks were considered state citizens. Under the Constitution, the federal courts have jurisdiction over a number of kinds of suits involving state citizens. Dred Scott's suit involved actions between citizens of different

states. The chief justice might have reasoned that free blacks in states
that considered them state citizens could bring certain kinds of suits in
federal courts.

Slavery The Fifth Amendment says that nobody may be "deprived
of life, liberty, or property, without due process of law." The chief justice reasoned that because slaves are "property," slaves cannot be taken
away without "due process of law." That is, slaves cannot be "taken
away" without a fair trial before an impartial court. According to the
chief justice, a law taking away slaves that have entered a free territory cheats slave owners of their due process rights. Thus the Missouri
Compromise was unconstitutional.

HOW DO BAD DECISIONS GET OVERRULED?

Historians generally consider *Dred Scott* to be the worst Supreme Court
decision of all time. Fortunately, this case is no longer good law. It has
been overruled. The Supreme Court has the power to overrule itself. A
constitutional amendment can also overrule a decision.

Dred Scott v. *Sanford* was so controversial that it hastened the coming of the Civil War. With the South defeated, Congress passed the 14th
Amendment (1868), which guaranteed African Americans citizenship
and overruled the *Dred Scott* decision.

QUESTION

1. How did Article III of the Constitution contradict Chief Justice Taney's conclusion that African Americans, whether slave or free, could not bring suits in federal
courts?

_____

_____

2. How might Taney's opinion have been different if the Supreme Court had ruled
that African Americans were entitled to the rights and privileges of citizens?

_____

_____

FIND OUT

What kinds of suits involving state citizens can federal courts hear?

Case 6: Civil Rights Cases (1883) Private Discrimination

THE ISSUE Under the Constitution, can Congress pass a law preventing private businesses from discriminating against people because of their race or color?

WHAT'S AT STAKE

Whether Americans can be discriminated against in their daily life.

FACTS AND BACKGROUND

After the Civil War (1861–1865), Congress passed the Civil Rights Act of 1875. The Act made it a crime to deny to anyone the "full and equal enjoyment" of railways and other transportation. It also required that all people be treated equally in hotels, theaters, and other places of public amusement. The law applied to people of every race and color, regardless of any previous condition of *servitude* [slavery]. Under the Act, privately owned businesses could not discriminate, either.

Some private business owners did not obey the law. They discriminated against African Americans. The U.S. Supreme Court combined and heard five such cases and issued one decision.

THE DECISION

The eight-member majority struck down the law. Justice Joseph P. Bradley wrote the opinion. In the Court's view, the 14th Amendment (which outlawed discrimination by a state) did not authorize the Act. "Individual invasion of individual rights is not the subject-matter of the amendment," Bradley wrote. "The wrongful act of an individual . . . is simply a private wrong." Congress could pass a law prohibiting a *state* from violating individual rights. It could not pass a law prohibiting private individuals or businesses from discriminating.

Bradley then turned to whether the 13th Amendment (which outlawed slavery) authorized the Act. Wasn't private discrimination against former slaves a *badge* [mark] of slavery? The Court said that it was not. Bradley's opinion added that such a broad reading of the 13th Amendment would make a freed former slave "the special favorite of the laws."

THE DISSENT

Justice John Marshall Harlan was the only dissenter. He said the majority was wrong. To Harlan, the 13th Amendment should be read broadly to give Congress the power to ensure the rights of freed people. Harlan said that private discrimination was a "badge of slavery" that Congress had a right to outlaw under the 13th Amendment. "It is not the words of the [amendment] but the internal sense of it that makes the law," he wrote. "The letter of the law is the body; the sense and reason of the law is the soul."

THE IMPACT OF THE DECISION

The decision helped usher in the "Jim Crow" era of discrimination against African Americans. (During the Jim Crow era, roughly the 1880s to the 1950s, African Americans, Hispanics, and Native Americans were segregated and suffered discrimination.) The justices said that *states* could outlaw discrimination, and some did eventually. But many states did not act. Businesses were free to discriminate. Not until the Civil Rights Act of 1964 did a federal law outlaw private discrimination.

HARLAN: THE GREAT DISSENTER

Justice John Marshall Harlan was a Kentuckian who had owned slaves. However, on the Court he became a great defender of equal treatment for all races. He wrote his blistering dissent in the *Civil Rights Cases* with the same pen and inkwell that Chief Justice Taney had used to write the *Dred Scott* decision. (Taney argued that African Americans had no rights. Harlan believed they had equal rights.) In *Plessy* v. *Ferguson* (1896) he was again the only dissenter.

QUESTION

1. What do you think Justice Harlan meant by "The letter of the law is the body; the sense and reason of the law is the soul"?

_____

_____

2. Do you think the amendment outlawing slavery also outlaws discrimination? Why or why not?

_____

_____

ONLINE EXTRA

Read the online case of *Heart of Atlanta Motel* v. *United States*. In it, the U. S. Supreme Court ruled on whether the Civil Rights Act of 1964 was constitutional. What did the Court decide? What was its reasoning? What provision of the Constitution did the Court base its decision on?

Case 7: Yick Wo v. Hopkins (1886)   Equal Protection

> **THE ISSUE** San Francisco denied licenses to Chinese laundries but gave licenses to laundries owned by non-Chinese. Did this violate the Equal Protection Clause of the Constitution?

WHAT'S AT STAKE

The rights of immigrants to equal protection of the laws. More broadly, whether the Equal Protection Clause can be used to strike down laws whose *effect* [result] is to discriminate.

FACTS AND BACKGROUND

In 1880, about 75,000 Chinese lived in California. They were almost 10 percent of the state's population. Many Californians did not like Chinese immigration to their state.

Nearly half of the state's Chinese lived in San Francisco. Because of restrictions on them, the Chinese tended to work in just a few jobs. About 90 percent of workers in laundries were Chinese. Almost all of them worked in wooden buildings. The city passed a law saying that laundries in wooden buildings had to be licensed by the Board of Supervisors. Laundries in brick or stone buildings did not have to be licensed. The reasoning was that wooden buildings were a fire hazard.

Yick Wo had been in the laundry business for more than 20 years, and his laundry had been inspected and found safe. Yet he and 200 other Chinese who applied for licenses were turned down. This meant that they could no longer do business. All but one of the 80 whites who applied were given licenses.

The law on its face made sense. If laundries in wooden buildings could burn down, it was reasonable to make sure that any laundry in a wooden building was safe. The question for the Court was whether the impact of the law when it was put into effect violated the Equal Protection Clause. Did the law, which did not seem to discriminate, actually discriminate when it was applied?

THE DECISION

Every member of the Court agreed that the law violated the Equal Protection Clause of the 14th Amendment, which says that all people must be protected equally by the law. Justice Stanley Mathews wrote for the Court. He pointed out that the 14th Amendment protects "persons," not just citizens. So even the Chinese who were not citizens have the right to the equal protection of the laws.

He then looked at the facts of the case, and concluded that the problem was not in how the law was *written*. It was in how the law was *applied*. Justice Matthews wrote that there was "no reason whatever, except the will of the supervisors," for selecting who got licenses and who did not. "The conclusion cannot be resisted that no reason for it exists except hostility to the race and nationality to which the [Chinese] belong. The discrimination is therefore illegal."

THE IMPACT OF THE DECISION

Though this law was struck down, the Chinese were still not welcome. In fact, Congress limited the immigration of Chinese in a number of laws. (Congress can lawfully limit the number of people who immigrate to the United States.)

The long-term effect of this decision was to set a precedent. A *precedent* guides courts as they make decisions in similar cases. In many civil rights cases, the Court looked at the *effect* of laws, not just how they were written. The Court began to use this analysis regularly around 1950 in such cases as *Brown* v. *Board of Education*. As a result, many laws were found to cause discrimination. The Court then struck them down.

QUESTIONS

1. Why did the Equal Protection Clause apply to the Chinese?

_____

_____

2. What do you think the Court would have decided if it just looked at the words of the law, and not the facts about who got licenses?

_____

_____

ONLINE EXTRA

In the case of *Plyler v. Doe* (1982), the Court had to decide another equal protection issue regarding immigrants. The issue was, can children of people who are in this country illegally attend public schools in Texas. Research the case online and report on what the Court decided, and why.

Case 8: Plessy v. Ferguson (1896) and Brown v. Board of Education (1954)

Equal Protection

THE ISSUES In *Plessy*, whether racially segregated railroad cars violate the Equal Protection Clause of the 14th Amendment. In *Brown*, whether racially segregated public schools violate that clause.

WHAT'S AT STAKE?

What "equal protection of the laws" means for all Americans.

FACTS AND BACKGROUND

The 14th Amendment is one of several amendments passed soon after the Civil War. These amendments were designed to guarantee the freedom of African Americans and to protect them from unfair treatment. The 14th Amendment's Equal Protection Clause reads: "No State shall . . . deny to any person within its jurisdiction the equal protection of the laws." But just what does this forbid? That's the key question for both cases.

Plessy v. *Ferguson* began in 1890 with a new Louisiana law. It said all railway companies in the state should provide "separate but equal" accommodations for white and African American passengers. To test the law, Homer Plessy refused to leave a white coach and was arrested. He argued that the law was unconstitutional.

Brown v. *Board of Education* began in 1950, when the National Association for the Advancement of Colored People tried to bring an end to segregation in the public schools. *Brown* included appeals from four separate states: Kansas, Delaware, South Carolina, and Virginia. School conditions in these four states varied. There were stark differences in South Carolina between the "colored" and "white" schools. In Topeka, Kansas, the schools were more equal. In all four states, however, the schools were segregated by law.

THE DECISIONS

Plessy v. Ferguson

In *Plessy*, the Supreme Court held that segregation was acceptable if the separate facilities provided for blacks were equal to those provided for whites. The sole dissent came from Justice Harlan. He said, "in the view of the Constitution, in the eye of the law, there is in this country no superior, dominant, ruling class of citizens.... Our constitution is color-blind, and neither knows nor tolerates classes among citizens." Justice Harlan accurately predicted further "aggressions, more or less brutal and irritating, upon the admitted rights of colored citizens."

Brown v. *Board of Education*

Chief Justice Earl Warren wrote the decision in *Brown* for a unanimous Court. He said that segregation of the public schools was unconstitutional. Even if the schools were equally new and the teachers equally paid, segregation in schools caused harm to African Americans. It marked them with a badge of inferiority. "We conclude that in the field of public education the doctrine of 'separate but equal' has no place," he wrote. "Separate educational facilities are inherently unequal."

THE IMPACT OF THE DECISIONS

Plessy created the legal doctrine of "separate but equal" that permitted racial segregation in the United States. African Americans and other people of color were sentenced to second-class citizenship. They were separated from whites in schools, stores, and restaurants.

Brown changed all that. It was a landmark in the struggle for equality under the law for all Americans. A few years after *Brown,* segregation by law was eliminated almost everywhere. It took more than 50 years, but eventually Justice Harlan's dissent became the law of the land.

QUESTIONS

1. What do you think Justice Harlan meant when he said that our Constitution is color blind?

_____

_____

2. What do you think Justice Warren meant when he wrote "Separate educational facilities are inherently unequal"?"

_____

_____

FIND OUT

1. In the 60 years between *Plessy* and *Brown*, were schools and other facilities actually equal?

2. Schools are no longer segregated by law, but are often segregated as a result of being located in segregated neighborhoods. Is that a problem for learning? If so, what can be done about it?

Case 9: Lochner v. New York (1905) Regulation of the Workplace

THE ISSUE Under the 14th Amendment, can a state limit the number of hours that employees may be required to work?

WHAT'S AT STAKE?

The case tested whether it was constitutional for states to regulate the hours people worked and other conditions of employment.

FACTS AND BACKGROUND

The New York legislature passed a law that said no bakery employee could work more than 60 hours in one week. The legislature thought that working long hours would hurt the workers' health. It thought that bosses were making workers agree to work long hours because the workers were afraid of losing their jobs.

Lochner, a bakery owner, was convicted of violating the law. He appealed his conviction. He said that the law was unconstitutional because it took away his liberty to make a contract about hours of labor with his employees. Lochner said that liberty of contract is promised by the 14th Amendment, which says that no state may "deprive any person of life, liberty, or property, without due process of law."

THE DECISION

By a narrow 5–4 margin, the Court agreed with Lochner. It struck down the law. The majority opinion was written by Justice Rufus Wheeler Peckham. He said the Constitution limited the police power of the state governments. *Police power* is a general power of a government to make regulations that support or protect the safety, health, morals and general welfare of its citizens. It is called "police power" because one of the meanings of the word *police* is "regulation."

Justice Peckham said that the Constitution permitted some interference with liberty of contract. In fact, the Court had approved a Utah law that said that nobody in an underground mine could work more than eight hours a day. Mining is clearly dangerous. Regulating it, Peckham said, was "fair, reasonable, and appropriate." But New York's interference with liberty of contract was "unreasonable, unnecessary, and arbitrary." (*Arbitrary* means decided randomly or on a whim.) Peckham said that the law was not necessary to protect health.

THE DISSENT

Four justices dissented from the ruling. Justice Oliver Wendell Holmes wrote, "This case is decided upon an economic theory which a large part of the country does not entertain," the theory of *laissez-faire*. (*Laissez-faire* is an economic theory that says the economy works best with as few regulations as possible.) But, said Holmes, "A Constitution is not intended to embody a particular economic theory. It is made for people of fundamentally differing views." Holmes wrote that the decision to regulate bakery workers was for the legislature, which had passed the law unanimously, and not for judges.

Many people agreed with Justice Holmes. State legislatures continued to make laws to protect workers. The Court struck down some of them, but permitted others.

THE COURT AND "SUBSTANTIVE DUE PROCESS"

The Fifth and 14th Amendments to the Constitution guarantee "due process of law." *Procedural* due process means that trials must be fair. *Substantive* due process focuses on the "life, liberty, or property" language of the Amendments. Judges who follow the theory of substantive due process believe that there are certain rights that government cannot interfere with unless there has been a fair trial. So someone may lose his liberty if found guilty by a court, but a legislature can't pass a law that takes away his liberty.

QUESTION

1. You are a member of the public. Do you approve of the New York bakery law? Explain your answer.

_____

_____

FIND OUT

1. Access the online discussion of *Muller* v. *Oregon* (1908). How was the Court's decision different from its decision in *Lochner*? Why did the Court decide this case as it did?

2. Research the laws to protect workers in your state. Describe three and how the laws protect workers.

3. Research and explain the difference between "substantive due process" and "procedural due process." Read the Fifth and 14th Amendments. Which type of due process do you think the Fifth and 14th Amendments were meant to protect?

Case 10: New Deal Cases
(1935, 1937)
Federal Regulation of Businesses

 THE ISSUE To what extent the Commerce Clause of the U.S. Constitution permits the federal government to regulate businesses?

WHAT'S AT STAKE?

The role of the states and the federal government in regulating business.

FACTS AND BACKGROUND

President Franklin D. Roosevelt and Congress tried to fight the Depression of the 1930s with many new programs and laws. This campaign to fight the Depression was called "The New Deal."

Congress felt it had authority to pass laws to improve the economy under the Constitution's Commerce Clause (Art. I, Sec. 8). Congress can regulate businesses that cross state lines, such as railroads and airlines, but can Congress regulate businesses that operate entirely within a state? Some people felt that these *intrastate* businesses could be regulated only by the state in which they were located.

The Supreme Court had to decide whether Congress had broad power to regulate businesses or a narrower power that applied only to certain types of businesses. The Court defined Congress's regulatory power in two important cases.

Schechter Poultry Corp. v. U.S.

The National Industrial Recovery Act (1933) was one of the first New Deal laws. In 1935, a case reached the Supreme Court that asked whether it was constitutional. The Schechter Poultry Company was accused of violating parts of the law that dealt with employees' pay and hours.

The company operated only in New York City. Though its poultry came from outside the state, the company said it was a local business. It argued that Congress did not have the power to make it pay employees a certain wage or give employees a set time off from work.

NLRB v. Jones and Laughlin Steel Corp.

In 1937, the Court was faced with another Commerce Clause case. The National Labor Relations Act guaranteed the right of workers to organize unions. A steel company was accused of violating the law. The company claimed that the Act should be thrown out because Congress did not have the authority under the Commerce Clause to pass it.

U.S. Supreme Court Case Studies

Case 10: New Deal Cases, *continued*   Federal Regulation of Businesses

THE DECISIONS

In the *Schechter* case, the Court agreed with the company and struck down the recovery law. In the *NLRB* case, it disagreed with the company and let the labor law stand.

The *Schechter* decision was unanimous. Chief Justice Charles Evans Hughes wrote the opinion. He said that the transactions in the case—wages and salaries and working hours—were local. These transactions did not have a "direct" effect on interstate commerce. The state could regulate such transactions, but the federal government could not.

In *NLRB*, the Court upheld the constitutionality of the labor law. The decision was 5–4. Chief Justice Hughes wrote for the majority. He said that the government could protect the right of workers to organize unions. Allowing workers to organize unions might prevent strikes that would hamper interstate commerce. Hughes dropped the distinction between "indirect" and "direct" effects on commerce made in *Schechter*. Under the *NLRB* ruling, an indirect effect would be enough to make a federal law governing interstate commerce constitutional.

THE IMPACT OF THE DECISIONS

Schechter was one of many decisions tossing out New Deal laws. In 1936, President Roosevelt was overwhelmingly re-elected. Early in 1937, he proposed a law that would add six new members to the Court. (Congress can change the number of justices.) This would enable him to appoint these six new justices. His proposal never became law, but in *NLRB*, the Court began to uphold New Deal laws.

Whatever the reason for the change, ever since its decision in *NLRB*, the Court has generally approved laws even indirectly affecting interstate commerce. This gives the federal government a great deal of power.

FIND OUT

1. Read about *Gibbons* v. *Ogden*. What did the Court say about the Commerce Clause there? Did that decision give more or less power to the federal government?

ONLINE EXTRA

Read the online discussion of *U.S.* v. *Lopez* (1995). What did the Court say about the Commerce Clause there? Did that decision give more or less power to the federal government?

Case 11: Korematsu v. U.S. (1944)   Racial Discrimination

> **THE ISSUE** Did the government violate the Equal Protection Clause of the 14th Amendment by singling out a racial group and forcing its members to leave their homes and move to camps hundreds of miles away?

WHAT'S AT STAKE?

For Japanese-Americans during World War II, whether they could be free of restrictions imposed only on them. More broadly, can the government use race directly and openly in making laws and rules?

FACTS AND BACKGROUND

In World War II, Japan fought on the side of Germany, Italy, and the Axis Powers. When the war began, about 112,000 Japanese-Americans lived on the West Coast; 70,000 of them were American citizens. After the United States entered the war in 1941, the U.S. military thought that these people might not be loyal to the U.S. In 1942, the military ordered most of the Japanese-Americans to move to special camps, called *internment camps*, far from their homes. The military was concerned they would commit sabotage and hurt the war effort.

Fred Korematsu, a Japanese-American and an American citizen, did not go to the camps as ordered. Korematsu was arrested and sent to an internment camp in Utah. He sued, claiming that the government acted illegally when it sent people of Japanese descent to camps.

THE DECISION

By a 6–3 margin, the Supreme Court said the orders were constitutional. Justice Hugo Black wrote the opinion for the Court. He said that the highly unusual demands of wartime security justified the orders. However, he made it clear that distinctions based on race are "inherently suspect." Laws and rules that are based on race must withstand "strict scrutiny" by the courts. "All legal restrictions which curtail the civil rights of a single racial group are immediately suspect. . . Pressing public necessity may sometime justify the existence of such restrictions; racial antagonism never can."

Justice Robert H. Jackson was one of the dissenters. He wrote that Korematsu was "convicted of an act not commonly a crime . . . being present in the state [where] he is a citizen . . . and where all his life he has lived." Jackson said the *Korematsu* decision was a "loaded weapon" that might be used again if the country is attacked.

Justice Frank Murphy also dissented. He said the military order reflected racial prejudice. He said the government should have conducted investigations to find out who was disloyal. It had done that with people of German and Italian ancestry. Instead, the government just rounded up almost everyone who was Japanese, without knowing who was loyal and who was not.

THE IMPACT OF THE CASE

The Japanese-Americans lost the case, but more than 40 years later, the U.S. passed a law that apologized to them. The law said that the government had been fundamentally unjust to have locked them up in camps. Thanks to the law, some Japanese-Americans received money to compensate them for what they had lost. In 1998, President Clinton awarded Fred Korematsu the National Medal of Freedom.

Though the case went against the Japanese, the strict scrutiny standard continues to guide the Court. *Strict scrutiny* means that using a suspect classification, such as race or gender, in a law would be unconstitutional unless the government can justify it as a *compelling* [very important] public interest. The government must also show that its action was narrowly tailored to advance this compelling interest. The strict scrutiny test is a very difficult standard for a law to meet. The Court has used this test in many cases, including the affirmative action cases *Gratz* v. *Bollinger* and *Grutter* v. *Bollinger*.

QUESTIONS

1. How did the Court justify the military orders that sent Japanese to camps? Do you agree with the Court?

_____

_____

2. What alternative did Justice Murphy prefer to the military order? Do you agree with him?

_____

_____

FIND OUT

1. Read about the affirmative action cases covered in this book. How did the Court in those cases apply the standards it had announced in *Korematsu*?

Case 12: Mapp v. Ohio (1961)

Search and Seizure

THE ISSUE Can evidence that police seized as a result of an illegal search be admitted in a state trial?

WHAT'S AT STAKE

Criminal *defendants* [people charged with a crime] are concerned whether state courts must exclude evidence that police seized illegally. This raises an important issue for all Americans—how can we enforce the Constitution when it does not specify a remedy if constitutional provisions are not followed?

FACTS AND BACKGROUND

The Fourth Amendment to the Constitution says Americans are "secure . . . against unreasonable searches and seizures." It doesn't say, however, exactly what an "unreasonable" search is. Nor does it say what happens when police find evidence as a result of an unreasonable search.

Searches aren't always reasonable. And sometimes illegal searches do turn up evidence that could help convict someone of a crime. At first, courts generally admitted illegally seized evidence. They reasoned that the individual's rights under the Fourth Amendment were secondary to the needs of justice. But that changed in a 1914 case, *Weeks* v. *United States*. The Supreme Court said that Weeks' Fourth Amendment rights had been violated by an illegal search. The Court held that the evidence could not be used against Weeks.

The *Weeks* decision set the standard for federal courts. The "exclusionary rule" announced in that case meant that illegally-seized evidence could not be used in federal courts. State courts were free to admit or not admit such evidence. The *Mapp* case asked whether state courts should follow the federal rule.

The case began when the police in Cleveland, Ohio, were looking for a fugitive suspected in a bombing case. They got a tip that he was hiding in Dollree Mapp's house. She refused to let them in. After surrounding the house, they broke down a door and began a search. They had a piece of paper that they claimed was a search warrant, but they didn't let her read it and didn't produce it later. They didn't find the fugitive, but in a trunk in the basement they found obscene material and jailed Mapp for that. She was convicted. She lost her appeal to the Ohio Supreme Court, though the court concluded that the search was "unlawful." Then she appealed to the U.S. Supreme Court.

U.S. Supreme Court Case Studies

THE DECISION

The Court ruled in favor of Mapp. The vote was 5-3. Justice Tom Clark wrote for the majority. "All evidence obtained by searches and seizures in violation of the Constitution is . . . inadmissible in a state court," he wrote. He said that the 14th Amendment's guarantee that states would not violate due process required that the exclusionary rule [that illegally seized evidence not be used] be applied to the states.

Justice John Marshall Harlan II (grandson of the great dissenter) wrote for the minority: "I would not impose upon the states this federal exclusionary remedy. . . The states should be free to follow it or not as they themselves determine."

THE IMPACT OF THE DECISION

The decision was controversial. It affected courts all over the United States. Many people were concerned that "[t]he criminal is to go free because the constable [police officer] has blundered." Others followed Justice Clark in saying, "The criminal goes free, if he must, but it is the law that sets him free. Nothing can destroy a government more quickly than its failure to observe its own laws."

QUESTIONS

1. Look at the Fourth Amendment and decide whether the search of Mapp's house was unreasonable. If so, what should have been done about it?

_____

_____

2. In the *Mapp* decision, Justice Clark said that there was "no war between the Constitution and common sense." What do you think he meant? Do you agree? Why or why not?

_____

_____

3. In your opinion, what is more important—protecting the individual's rights or protecting society? Explain your answer.

_____

_____

Case 13: Baker v. Carr (1962)   One Person, One Vote

THE ISSUE Does the Supreme Court have jurisdiction over cases that raise the issue of how states create legislative districts?

WHAT'S AT STAKE

How state legislative districts are drawn affects who gets elected and which laws get passed. The broader question is whether courts should get involved in "political" questions.

FACTS AND BACKGROUND

In all states, legislators are elected from districts. Each district usually elects one representative to the legislature. The districts must be redrawn every 10 years to reflect changes in the population. What happens when some districts contain many voters and some only a few?

The Tennessee constitution required redrawing of the districts every ten years. However, in 1960, Tennessee had not redrawn its legislative boundaries since 1901. The cities and suburbs had grown, but they still elected a small number of representatives. The rural areas had lost population, but they still elected most of the legislature. The votes of people in rural areas counted for more than the votes of city people. Some people thought this discriminated against city people.

Voters from Tennessee cities sued the state in federal court. They said their votes had less weight, violating the Equal Protection Clause of the 14th Amendment. That clause says that no state shall deny to any person "the equal protection of the laws." The federal court dismissed the suit. The voters appealed to the U.S. Supreme Court.

THE DECISION

The Supreme Court had to decide if the federal courts had authority to hear the case. By a 6-2 margin (one justice did not participate), the Court said that they did. The case could go forward. Writing for the majority, Justice William Brennan wrote that the equal protection issues raised in this case merited evaluation by the courts. [The voters bringing the suit] "are entitled to a trial and a decision" on whether they were denied equal protection. He said that courts had long experience applying the Equal Protection Clause. There were "well developed and familiar standards" to guide them.

Justices John Marshall Harlan and Felix Frankfurter dissented. They said that the Equal Protection Clause did not require "that state legislatures must be so structured as to reflect with approximate equality the voice of every voter." To them, the claim of discrimination was not valid. The voters were merely being deprived of their share of political influence. Any new or redrawn districts would still favor some groups over others.

The dissenters also urged that courts not get tangled in "political thickets." Instead, the federal courts should defer to "the judgment of state legislatures and courts on matters of basically local concern."

THE IMPACT OF THE DECISION

Baker v. Carr had a huge impact. Chief Justice Warren wrote that it was "the most vital decision" handed down in his years on the Court. Within nine months of the decision, at least 34 states were facing suits for reapportionment. All eventually were redistricted.

In 1963, in *Grey* v. *Sanders*, the Court announced the standard of "one man, one vote." This required that the weight of votes be as equal as possible. Writing for the Court, Chief Justice Warren said, "legislators represent people, not trees or acres." In later cases, the Supreme Court ruled that the one-person, one-vote principle must be the primary consideration in drawing up districts for both houses of state legislatures. It also must be the standard for how each state divides its districts for the U.S. Congress.

QUESTIONS

1. Do you agree with the majority in this case, or with the dissenters? Why?

_____

_____

2. What does the Constitution say about drawing up Congressional districts (Article 1, Section 2)? How does this differ from the Senate? (Article 1, Section 3)?

_____

_____

FIND OUT

How was your state apportioned before *Baker* v. *Carr*? Was population the basis for one house of your legislature, and something else—such as the same number of legislators for each county—the basis for the other house?

Case 14: Engel v. Vitale (1962)   School Prayer

 THE ISSUE Does a state violate the First Amendment when it composes a prayer that students are to say at the beginning of each school day?

WHAT'S AT STAKE?

In the case itself, the future of organized prayer in the schools. The broader issue is the proper role of government toward religion under the First Amendment.

FACTS AND BACKGROUND

The state of New York recommended that public schools in the state begin the day by having students recite a prayer. It wrote a brief prayer for them to say: "Almighty God, we acknowledge our dependence upon Thee, and we beg Thy blessing upon us, our parents, our teachers, and our country."

A group of parents sued to stop the official prayer. They said it was contrary to their beliefs and the beliefs of their children. They said the state law was unconstitutional. The First Amendment says that "Congress shall make no law respecting an establishment of religion." This is known as the "establishment clause." The First Amendment applies to the states through the 14th Amendment.

The parents argued that the state illegally preferred religion to nonreligion. They said this amounted to "establishing" [officially supporting] religion. Though students were permitted to remain silent, the parents claimed that inevitably there would be pressure on them to participate.

The state replied that no one was forced to say the prayer. It didn't involve spending any public money. It didn't establish religion. In fact, it encouraged freedom to worship. The state pointed out that the First Amendment requires that: "Congress shall make no law prohibiting the free exercise [of religion]." This is known as the "free exercise clause."

THE DECISION

By a 6-1 margin (two justices did not take part in the case), the Court agreed with the parents. It struck down the state law. Justice Hugo Black wrote for the majority. He pointed out that the prayer was clearly religious. He said the First Amendment "must at least mean that in this country it is no part of the business of government to compose official prayers for any group of American people to recite as part of a religious program carried on by government."

27   U.S. Supreme Court Case Studies

His decision looked at the thinking of the Founders, especially Jefferson and Madison. Black said, "These men knew that the First Amendment, which tried to put an end to governmental control of religion and prayer, was not written to destroy either."

Justice Potter Stewart was the only dissenter. He wrote, "I cannot see how an 'official religion' is established by letting those who want to say a prayer say it." He pointed out that the Supreme Court begins each day when one of its officials invokes the protection of God. The Senate and House of Representatives open each day with a prayer. He argued that the New York prayer was similar to these traditions. It permitted students to share in "the spiritual heritage of our Nation."

THE IMPACT OF THE DECISION

This decision was very controversial. Many people felt it was against religion. A year later, in *Abington School District* v. *Schempp* (1963), the Court issued another controversial ruling. It struck down beginning the school day with a Bible reading. Later cases have struck down posting the Ten Commandments in the classroom and a moment of silence for prayer, as well as prayers at graduation. Many attempts have been made to change the Constitution to permit prayer in public schools, but none have been successful. *Engel* v. *Vitale* remains the law of the land.

QUESTIONS

1. Read the First Amendment. Do you think it forbids organized prayer in the schools? Why or why not?

_____

_____

2. James Madison wrote "it is proper to take alarm at the first experiment on our liberties." What do you think he meant by that? Is saying an official prayer in school the first step toward "establishing" religion? Explain your answer.

_____

_____

FIND OUT

If the Senate and House of Representatives begin each day with prayer, why are schools prevented from beginning with organized prayer? Is there something special about schools that makes prayer there different?

Case 15: Gideon v. Wainwright (1963)   Right to a Lawyer

THE ISSUE Under the Constitution, is a poor person accused of a serious crime guaranteed the free assistance of a lawyer?

WHAT'S AT STAKE?

For the thousands of poor people accused of crime each year, the right to have a more even playing field with the prosecution.

FACTS AND BACKGROUND

Clarence Earl Gideon was accused of breaking and entering into a Florida poolroom and stealing money. When Gideon's case came to trial he could not afford to hire a lawyer. He asked that the court supply him with one for free. The judge refused. Gideon conducted his own defense but was found guilty. While in prison, Gideon handwrote a document called a writ. It asked the U. S. Supreme Court to review his case. He claimed that by refusing to appoint a lawyer to help him, the Florida court had violated his right to a lawyer.

Because of his poverty, the Supreme Court allowed him to file his document for free. When the Court accepted the case, it appointed a lawyer to represent him before the Court. His lawyer was Abe Fortas, who later became a Supreme Court justice.

Fortas argued that the Sixth Amendment, which guarantees people the right to a lawyer in criminal trials, applied to the states because of the 14th Amendment. The 14th Amendment says that no state "shall deprive any person of life, liberty, or property without due process of law." ("Due process" includes trial by jury and other procedures that make trials fair.) Fortas said that depriving Gideon of a lawyer made his trial unfair and violated his right to due process.

THE DECISION

By a 9-0 margin, the Court agreed with Gideon. Justice Hugo Black wrote for the Court. He pointed out that the Sixth Amendment says that "the accused shall enjoy the right . . . to have the Assistance of Counsel [a lawyer] for his defense." The Sixth Amendment applies to the federal courts. The Supreme Court had held in previous cases that defendants in federal court had to have a free lawyer if they wanted one. Many states had passed laws giving accused people the right to a free lawyer. In this decision, the Court held that, because of the 14th Amendment, all states must make free lawyers available. Justice Black

U.S. Supreme Court Case Studies

said that it was an "obvious truth" that "assistance of counsel" is necessary for a fair trial in any court.

Black pointed out that "governments . . . spend vast sums of money . . . to [prosecute] defendants." If we are to achieve the goal that "every defendant stands equal before the law," then we must recognize that defendants need lawyers to present their side of the case and balance the scales of justice. In Black's words, "lawyers in criminal court are necessities, not luxuries." Gideon got a new trial, with a lawyer to defend him. The lawyer was able to call new witnesses and cast doubt on the prosecution's witnesses. Gideon was acquitted in this trial.

THE IMPACT OF THE DECISION

Gideon was one of several Supreme Court cases that extended the right to a lawyer. One said that lawyers had to be made available even in trials for minor crimes (misdemeanors) that might involve jail time. The Court held in another case that free lawyers must be available to help defendants pursue their right to appeal their conviction.

Today, all states either have public defenders who defend poor people or have a system where courts appoint a lawyer for each defendant who needs one. Some people say that the playing field is still uneven. Prosecutors' offices are generally larger and have more resources than public defender offices. Nonetheless, now no defendant has to go to court without a lawyer.

QUESTIONS

1. What does the Sixth Amendment say about the right to a lawyer? Do you think these words require free lawyers for poor people accused of a crime? How else does the Sixth Amendment help assure fair trials?

   _____

   _____

2. What does the 14th Amendment say about due process? Does due process require free lawyers for poor people accused of a crime?

   _____

   _____

Case 16: Miranda v. Arizona (1966)   Right to Remain Silent

> **THE ISSUE** Does the Constitution require police to tell people in custody of their right to remain silent and their right to an attorney?

WHAT'S AT STAKE?

Constitutional requirements that police everywhere must follow.

FACTS AND BACKGROUND

In 1963, a woman was kidnapped in Arizona. Ernesto Miranda was arrested for the crime and taken to the police station. He was 23 years old, poor, and had limited education. The officers took Miranda to a room to question him. After a short time, he gave a detailed confession.

At Miranda's trial, the officers testified that Miranda had given the confession without any threats or force. The officers admitted that they had not told Miranda about his rights to silence or legal assistance. Miranda was found guilty and sentenced to a long prison term. After the Arizona Supreme Court upheld his conviction, Miranda appealed to the United States Supreme Court.

THE DECISION

By a bare 5-4 majority, the Supreme Court ruled that taking Miranda's confession without informing him of his rights to silence and legal assistance had deprived him of rights promised to him by the Fifth and Sixth Amendments.

Chief Justice Earl Warren wrote for the majority. He pointed out that the Fifth Amendment says that no person "shall be compelled in any criminal case to be a witness against himself." This means that defendants in a criminal case can't be required to testify at their trial. The issue here was whether the Fifth Amendment requires police to inform people of their right to remain silent when they were in police custody.

Warren's opinion held that it did. He noted that the "very fact of custodial interrogation exacts a heavy toll . . . and trades on the weakness of individuals." *Custodial* means that someone is arrested, or at least "deprived of his freedom of action in any significant way."

Warren also wrote that not informing Miranda of his right to have legal help had deprived him of his Sixth Amendment right to "have the assistance of counsel for his defense." Miranda also had the right to know that he had the right to a free lawyer if he could not afford one. So to meet the requirements of the Fifth and Sixth Amendments, people in custody would have to be told of their rights. Police now do this routinely.

If police fail to give the Miranda warnings, judges will rule that what people in custody tell the police may not be used as evidence against them in court, nor can any evidence police find that was based on what the prisoner said. Other evidence may be used in court, such as the testimony of witnesses. In fact, at his second trial, Miranda was convicted on other evidence.

THE IMPACT OF THE DECISION

Miranda was one of the most controversial cases in Supreme Court history. Many people thought that the result would make it harder to convict people because fewer people would confess. However, studies have shown that confession rates have changed little because of the decision.

THE MIRANDA WARNINGS

Anyone who has seen TV cop shows has heard some variation of these warnings over and over again. All are based on the *Miranda* decision. They may differ slightly from place to place. Here is a sample:

1. You have the right to remain silent;

2. Anything you say can and will be used against you;

3. You have the right to talk to a lawyer before being questioned and to have a lawyer present when you are being questioned; and

4. If you can't afford a lawyer, one will be provided for you before any questioning if you want one.

QUESTIONS

1. What rights of the individual does the Fifth Amendment protect? The Sixth Amendment?

_____

_____

2. Do you think giving a Miranda warning helps protect those rights? Why or why not?

_____

_____

Case 17: Tinker v. Des Moines (1969)

Free Expression for Students

 THE ISSUE Under the First Amendment, can school officials prohibit students from wearing armbands to symbolize political protest?

WHAT'S AT STAKE

The extent to which all American public school students can take part in political protests in their schools.

FACTS AND BACKGROUND

Some students in Des Moines, Iowa, decided to wear black armbands to protest the Vietnam War. Two days before the protest, the school board created a new policy. It stated that any student who wore an armband to school and refused to remove it would be suspended.

Three students wore armbands and were suspended. They said that their First Amendment right to freedom of speech had been violated. They sued the Des Moines Independent Community School District. In 1969, the United States Supreme Court decided their case.

THE DECISION

By a 7-2 margin, the Court agreed with the students. Justice Abe Fortas wrote for the majority. He said that students do not "shed their constitutional rights to freedom of speech . . . at the schoolhouse gate."

Fortas admitted that school officials had the right to set rules. However, their rules had to be consistent with the First Amendment. That Amendment states that "Congress shall make no law . . . abridging [limiting] the freedom of speech." The Court had held in previous cases that under the 14th Amendment, state and local governments (including school boards) must follow the First Amendment.

Fortas's opinion held that wearing an armband symbolizing political protest was a form of speech called symbolic speech. Symbolic speech is conduct that expresses an idea. Even though the protest did not involve spoken words (called pure speech), it did express an opinion. It was a form of expression protected in the same way as pure speech.

The Court had said in previous cases that free speech does not mean that someone may speak anywhere, at any time, or in any way. You can't turn a loud speaker to full volume and wake up a neighborhood at four in the morning. In this case, Des Moines school officials thought their rule was justified. They feared that the protest would disrupt learning.

U.S. Supreme Court Case Studies

Fortas wrote that student symbolic speech could be punished, but only if it really disrupts education. In actuality, only a few students out of 18,000 wore armbands. There was little or no disruption. Fortas wrote that officials couldn't pass a rule out of a general fear of disruption. Unpopular views may create unpleasantness. That's part of living in a free society.

Fortas also noted that the officials allowed students to wear other political symbols, such as political campaign buttons. By singling out armbands, officials appeared to stifle a particular point of view. Courts are suspicious of rules that seem to target a particular message.

THE IMPACT OF THE CASE

Tinker remains the law of the land, but later cases, with different facts, often have permitted school officials to exercise more control. In *Hazelwood School District* v. *Kuhlmeier* (1988), the Court upheld a school principal who had removed two pages from a student newspaper before it was published. He was concerned that the pages violated the privacy of some students. The First Amendment guarantees freedom of press. However, the Court noted that students don't automatically have the rights adults do in other settings. The school newspaper was part of a journalism course and was sponsored by the school. As a result, educators "are entitled to exercise greater control . . . to assure that participants learn whatever lessons the activity is designed to teach." The tensions between constitutional guarantees and the special circumstances of schools will continue to be played out in future cases.

QUESTION

1. Should teenagers in school have as much freedom of speech as adults? Why or why not?

_____

_____

ONLINE EXTRA

What did the Court decide in *Bethel School District* v. *Fraser* (1986)? How did its decision in *Bethel* compare to its decision in *Hazelwood School District* v. *Kuhlmeier*? Do you agree with the Court's decisions? Explain your answer.

Case 18: New York Times v. United States (1971)

Freedom of Press

THE ISSUE Under the First Amendment, can the government stop a newspaper, in wartime, from publishing articles that the government claims are harmful to national security?

WHAT'S AT STAKE?

Whether the New York Times could continue to publish articles that were critical of the government's conduct during the Vietnam War. The broader issue is when, if ever, the government has the right to prevent a story from being published.

FACTS AND BACKGROUND

In 1971, the country was bitterly divided over the Vietnam War. Some people in the Defense Department had access to classified documents. The documents showed that secrecy and deception marked the beginnings of the Vietnam War. Daniel Ellsberg gave the documents, which became known as the Pentagon Papers, to the New York Times. The newspaper began to publish a series of stories based on the Pentagon Papers.

After the third article was published, the federal government tried to stop the newspaper from finishing the series. This is called *prior restraint*. Prior restraint is when the government tries to stop the publication of something before it is published.

The case moved very rapidly. The government asked a court for a temporary restraining order that would halt publication. The court granted the order and stopped publication of the articles. The newspaper appealed immediately. Because of the national importance of the case, the Supreme Court agreed to bypass the appeals court. The Supreme Court heard the case a few days later. Four days after that, the Court issued its decision.

THE DECISION

By a 6-3 majority, the Court denied the government's request for an order stopping publication. Quoting previous cases, the Court said that "any system of prior restraints of expression comes to this Court bearing a heavy presumption against its constitutional validity." The government "carries a heavy burden of showing justification for the imposition of such a restraint." The Court held that in this case the government had not met its burden. The articles could be published.

U.S. Supreme Court Case Studies

The six justices in the majority had differing reasoning. Three justices said that the courts should never allow the government to stop publication. They said that the First Amendment is very clear. Under it, "the press must be left free to publish news, whatever the source, without censorship, injunctions or prior restraints." To give the government the power to stop publication would "wipe out the First Amendment and destroy the fundamental liberty and security of the very people the government hopes to make secure."

Three other justices said that prior restraint was not justified in this case. However, they wouldn't go so far as to say that it was never justified. They noted that the government understandably wanted these documents not to be published. Yet they felt that the documents, though embarrassing to the government, were not harmful to national security.

The three dissenters said that the First Amendment does not guarantee an absolute right to publish. They pointed out that Article II of the Constitution gives the president powers in foreign affairs, which should include the power to prevent stolen documents from being published. They also noted the case had been very rushed, and that the Court did not have enough time to fully decide the merits of the controversy. Finally, they pointed out that materials used for the stories were stolen and given to the newspaper, which raised issues under criminal law.

THE IMPACT OF THE DECISION

The articles continued to be published. The government tried unsuccessfully to prosecute Daniel Ellsberg, but the prosecution was not successful. In the end, the case was a victory for freedom of the press.

QUESTIONS

1. Read the First Amendment. Do you think it forbids all prior restraint? Explain your answer.

_____

_____

2. Do you think that the government should have the power of prior restraint in some circumstances? If so, when? Explain your answer.

_____

_____

Case 19: Privacy Cases (1965, 1973, 1990) Right to Privacy

THE ISSUES Under the Constitution, can the government interfere in very personal decisions, such as decisions about contraceptives, abortion, and when and how to die?

WHAT'S AT STAKE?

The right of an individual to make very personal and private decisions that may involve life or death.

FACTS AND BACKGROUND

Each of the cases raises different specific issues. However, each case deals with the extent to which the state can regulate what people do with their bodies.

In *Griswold* v. *Connecticut* (1965), the issue was whether a Connecticut law was constitutional. That law made it illegal for a person to use any drug or article to prevent conception or pregnancy. In *Roe* v. *Wade* (1973), the issue was whether a Texas law that severely restricted abortions was constitutional. In *Cruzan* v. *Missouri Department of Health* (1990), the issue was whether the state could prevent a comatose woman's parents from refusing life-sustaining treatment for her. *Comatose* means that the person is not conscious and is in a coma.

THE DECISIONS

Griswold The Court struck down the Connecticut law by a 7-2 margin. Justice William O. Douglas wrote that several amendments—including the First, Third, Fourth and Fifth—implied that the Constitution protected "zones of privacy." (Justice Douglas did not find a right to privacy specifically expressed in the Constitution.) The Connecticut law was unconstitutional because it violated the privacy of married persons.

Justices Stewart and Black dissented. Stewart said the law was "uncommonly silly." However, he did not think it went against a fundamental constitutional right. Black complained that finding new rights, such as the "zones of privacy," in the Constitution amounted to a "day-to-day constitutional convention." Black said that such an interpretation is "bad for the courts and worse for the country."

Roe The Court struck down the Texas law by a 7-2 margin. Justice Harry Blackmun wrote for the majority. He said that the law violated the Constitution's right to privacy. Blackmun found the privacy right in the Due Process Clause of the 14th Amendment: no state shall "deprive

any person of life, liberty, or property, without due process of law."
Therefore, the state could regulate abortions only later in the pregnancy,
to protect the health of the woman or the life of the fetus.

Justices Byron White and William Rehnquist dissented. They said
the state had a right to protect the potential life of the fetus all the way
through the pregnancy. They pointed out that many states had laws
against abortion when the 14th Amendment was adopted in 1868. No
one at that time thought the Amendment made them unconstitutional.

Cruzan By a 5-4 margin, the Court upheld Missouri's rules. Under
these rules, Nancy Cruzan's parents were prevented from removing her
life support systems unless Nancy had earlier clearly expressed such
a preference. Chief Justice Rehnquist wrote the majority opinion. He
said that in protecting "liberty," the Due Process Clause gave patients a
constitutional right to refuse treatment. But Rehnquist felt that the state
was within its constitutional rights to demand that the patient—Nancy
Cruzan, not her parents—have expressed the refusal clearly.

Justice Brennan wrote the main dissent. He agreed that the Due
Process Clause gives people the right to avoid unwanted medical
treatment. But since Nancy Cruzan's right to refuse treatment "is not
outweighed by any interests of the State, I respectfully dissent. Nancy
Cruzan is entitled to choose to die with dignity."

THE IMPACT OF THE DECISIONS

Roe had a huge effect. It overturned laws against abortion in every state.
The decision was—and still is—very controversial. Later cases have
upheld *Roe*, but have also given states a little more room to regulate
when and how doctors can perform abortions. As for *Cruzan*, courts
and legislatures are still working through "right to die" issues.

QUESTION

1. Read the First, Third, Fourth and Fifth amendments. Do they suggest that the
   Founders meant to protect privacy? Why or why not?

_____

FIND OUT

Read about *Lochner* v. *New York*. In that case, the Court held that the
14th Amendment prevented the state from regulating the hours of bak-
ers. Is the reasoning in *Roe* similar? What do you think about using the
general language of this amendment to strike down laws?

Case 20: United States v. Nixon (1974)   Executive Privilege

THE ISSUE Does the Constitution give the president an absolute right to keep certain information private?

WHAT'S AT STAKE

The investigation of the Watergate scandal was at stake. So was the future of Richard Nixon's presidency. The broader issue was to what extent presidents have an "executive privilege" to keep some information completely private.

FACTS AND BACKGROUND

In 1972, burglars were caught breaking into the headquarters of the Democratic National Committee at the Watergate Hotel. Their mission was to install "bugs" for listening in on the Democratic party's telephone conversations. The burglars were linked to President Richard Nixon's re-election campaign organization.

As Congress investigated the break-in in 1973, many witnesses claimed that the president was trying to cover up his involvement. One witness revealed that Nixon had secretly tape-recorded every conversation that had ever taken place in his office.

By April 1974, criminal charges had been filed against seven members of Nixon's administration. The special prosecutor in the case asked Nixon to let him hear the tapes. Nixon refused. The prosecutor asked the federal district court for help. The judge ordered Nixon to release the tapes to the court for secret examination. Nixon disobeyed. This caused a constitutional crisis—a tug of war between two branches of government. Could a president defy a federal judge?

Nixon claimed that as president, he had an executive privilege of keeping presidential communications confidential. Nobody could override it for any reason. Nixon claimed that a president had a right to refuse to testify in court or provide information requested by other branches of government. The right of executive privilege is not mentioned in the Constitution. For years presidents had claimed a right to it in foreign relations for national security reasons.

Because of the urgency of the case, the United State Supreme Court agreed to skip over the Court of Appeals, which would normally have heard the first appeal, and settle the case right away.

THE DECISION

The decision was unanimous. Chief Justice Warren Burger wrote for the Court. He said that the president's executive privilege is not absolute. Nixon had to turn over the tapes.

Nixon had argued that the separation of powers requires the executive and judicial branches to be totally independent. The chief justice rejected this claim. Under the separation of powers, the Constitution gives each branch a job of its own to do. If the president could withhold evidence from the courts, the courts could not do the job the Constitution gave them.

Nixon's second argument was that communications between the president and his advisers need to be confidential for the sake of the public good. Burger admitted that sometimes confidentiality, or secretiveness, is important. When communications are about diplomatic or military secrets, confidentiality might be necessary. But when communications concern other subjects, confidentially might not be important at all. Burger concluded that the need for confidentiality must be balanced against competing needs on a case-by-case basis.

In this case, said Burger, finding the truth requires that courts have all the evidence they need, even if it includes presidential communications. When the need to find out the truth in the Watergate trial was weighed against President Nixon's need for confidentiality, confidentiality lost.

THE IMPACT OF THE DECISION

Nixon turned over the tapes. The evidence on the tapes showed that he had been part of the cover-up. As a result, Nixon had to resign. The long-run impact is that the Court set some guidelines. It clearly said that there is no such thing as an absolute executive privilege. The president's need for confidentiality must be weighed against competing needs, such as the needs of the criminal justice system. In disputed cases, federal courts may do this weighing.

QUESTION

1. "Executive privilege" is mentioned nowhere in the Constitution. Was the Court right to say that other words in the Constitution gave this power to presidents? Why or why not?

_____

_____

Case 21: Texas v. Johnson (1989)

Flag-Burning

THE ISSUE Does the First Amendment protect burning the U.S. flag as a form of symbolic speech?

WHAT'S AT STAKE?

Determining the limits of symbolic speech, especially in regard to one of our national symbols.

FACTS AND BACKGROUND

At the 1984 Republican National Convention in Texas, Gregory Lee Johnson doused a U.S. flag with kerosene and burned the flag. He did this as a form of protest. A Texas law made it a crime to *desecrate* [treat disrespectfully] the national flag. Johnson was convicted of violating this law. He was sentenced to one year in prison and fined $2,000.

The Texas Court of Criminal Appeals reversed the conviction. The court maintained that Johnson's burning of the flag was actually a form of symbolic speech. Therefore, the First Amendment protected it. Texas then appealed to the U.S. Supreme Court.

It was up to the Supreme Court to decide the validity of Johnson's conviction. The First Amendment says, "Congress shall make no law . . . abridging the freedom of speech." What actions, however, can be included under the term speech? According to the Texas Court of Criminal Appeals, burning a flag could be protected speech. The court stated, "Given the context of an organized demonstration . . . anyone who observed . . . would have understood the message . . . [The flag burning] was clearly 'speech' [under] the First Amendment . . ." The state of Texas, however, argued that it had an interest in preserving the flag as a symbol of national unity and preventing disruptions.

THE DECISION

The Court ruled for Johnson. The vote was very close, five to four. Justice Brennan wrote for the majority. He said that Johnson was within his constitutional rights when he burned the U.S. flag in protest.

As in *Tinker* v. *Des Moines Independent Community School District*, the Court looked at the First Amendment and symbolic speech. Brennan concluded that Johnson's act was "expressive conduct." He was trying to "convey a . . . message." Thus, his burning the flag as a form of symbolic speech—like the students wearing armbands in Des Moines in their political protest—is protected by the First Amendment. According to Brennan, "Government may not prohibit the expression of an idea [because it is] offensive."

Answering the state of Texas' arguments, Brennan said that Johnson's act posed no threat of disruption. Also, burning the flag did not endanger its status as a national symbol. As a result, the Court declared the Texas law unconstitutional.

Chief Justice Rehnquist dissented. He quoted poetry to show how much Americans love the flag. He said the flag is "the visible symbol embodying our Nation. It does not represent the views of any particular political party, and it does not represent any particular political philosophy. The flag is not simply another 'idea' or 'point of view' competing for recognition in the marketplace of ideas."

THE IMPACT OF THE DECISION

Critics of the Court's ruling in *Texas* v. *Johnson* argued that the Court had interpreted the term "speech" too broadly. Many people were deeply offended that flag burning could go unpunished. In direct response to the Court's controversial ruling, the U.S. Congress passed the Flag Protection Act of 1989. The Supreme Court ruled this act unconstitutional in *The United States* v. *Eichman* in June 1990.

Thus the only way to overturn the decision is through a constitutional amendment. Many amendments banning flag burning have been proposed, but none, so far, has become part of the Constitution.

QUESTION

1. In your own words, explain what Justice Brennan meant when he said "We do not consecrate the flag by punishing its desecration, for in doing so we dilute the freedom that this cherished emblem represents." Do you agree with Brennan? Why or why not?

_____

_____

ONLINE EXTRA

The First Amendment permits some restrictions on speech. Read the online discussion of *Schenck* v. *United States* (1919). Why was speech limited in that case? Take a look at *United States* v. *American Library Association* (2003). What limits, if any, did the Court place on speech in that case?

Case 22: Bush v. Gore (2000)

Presidential Election

THE ISSUE Should 60,000 ballots that could not be read by voting machines be recounted by hand to determine whether a voter intended to cast a vote for George W. Bush or Al Gore in the 2000 election?

WHAT'S AT STAKE?

The presidency of the United States. The question was whether George Bush or Al Gore won the 2000 presidential election. The broader issues are the ability of the Supreme Court to overrule the decisions of state courts on state laws, and the ability of an appointed judiciary to affect the result of democratic elections.

FACTS AND BACKGROUND

The presidential election between Democrat Gore and Republican Bush on November 7, 2000, was very close. Whoever won the state of Florida would be the next president.

People voted in Florida by punching a hole in a ballot card. The votes were then counted by a machine, which detected the holes. The machines in Florida showed that Bush had won the state by a few hundred votes. On November 26, Florida's Election Commission declared the election in favor of Bush.

However, 60,000 ballots were not counted because the machines could not detect a hole in the voting card. In some of these ballots, there was an indentation or "dimple" where the voter tried to punch a hole. In other ballots, a voter had almost made a hole, and there was a piece of paper, or "hanging chad," hanging from the hole. Al Gore argued in the Florida Supreme Court that these votes, called *under-votes*, should be recounted by hand. On December 8, 2000, the Florida Supreme Court agreed and ordered counties to recount all under-votes. If a voter's intent to choose Bush or Gore could be clearly determined from the ballot, then the vote would be added to the totals for Bush or Gore.

Bush appealed to the United States Supreme Court on December 9. The Court made an order to stop the recounts while it made a decision. The Court handed down a decision on December 12, 2000.

THE DECISION

The Supreme Court voted 5-4 to end the hand recount of under-votes ordered by the Florida Supreme Court.

The majority pointed out that the Florida Supreme Court had ordered a recount without giving much guidance to vote-counters on

U.S. Supreme Court Case Studies

what was a valid vote. Some counters counted votes on dimpled ballots; some only counted votes with hanging chads. The Supreme Court said that the inconsistency in methods of counting votes meant that votes were treated *arbitrarily* [based on a person's choice, rather than on standards]. This lack of standards, said the Court, violated the Due Process and Equal Protection Clauses of the Constitution.

Five justices said that under Florida law, the vote had to be finalized by December 12. They said that rules for re-counts could not be properly formulated in that time, and so they ordered election officials to stop re-counting votes.

In a highly unusual move, the majority in the unsigned 5-4 decision said that this case should not be used as precedent in future cases: "Our consideration is limited to the present circumstances, for the problem of equal protection in election processes involves many complexities."

In one dissent, Justices David Souter and Stephen Breyer agreed with the majority that the lack of standards on what votes to count meant that the re-counting process was not valid. However, they thought Florida courts should have a chance to create standards so that a recount could be conducted before the Electoral College met on December 18. In another dissent, Justices John Paul Stevens and Ruth Bader Ginsburg said that the decision of the Florida Supreme Court was reasonable, and that the U.S. Supreme Court should respect it.

THE IMPACT OF THE DECISION

As a result of the Supreme Court's decision, George W. Bush received Florida's electoral votes, and was declared President-elect of the United States on December 18, 2000.

QUESTION

1. Why did the majority in the U.S. Supreme Court believe that the Florida Supreme Court's order was unconstitutional?

_____

_____

FIND OUT

Did an unelected body ever before decide a presidential election? If so, when? What was the result?

Case 23: Gratz v. Bollinger and Grutter v. Bollinger (2003)

Affirmative Action

THE ISSUE Did a university violate the Constitution by considering race when admitting students to its undergraduate school and law school?

WHAT'S AT STAKE?

The future of affirmative action programs in higher education.

FACTS AND BACKGROUND

Jennifer Gratz and Barbara Grutter are both white. They challenged the University of Michigan's affirmative action admissions policies. The university has these policies to help assure a *diversified* [varied] group of students. Gratz said that the university violated the Constitution by considering race as a factor in its undergraduate admissions programs. Grutter claimed that the University of Michigan Law School also did so.

The undergraduate program automatically gave one-fifth of the points needed to guarantee admission to every minority applicant from an underrepresented group. (*Underrepresented* means a group attending the college at a rate less than its numbers in society.) They got this solely because of minority status. The law school's admissions policy was different. It didn't give all minority candidates extra points simply because they were members of a minority group. Instead, the law school looked at each applicant individually. It considered each applicant's talents, experiences, and potential. It also did not define diversity only in terms of racial and ethnic status.

THE DECISIONS

The cases were decided on the same day. In *Gratz*, the Court ruled 6-3 that the undergraduate program was unconstitutional. Chief Justice Rehnquist's opinion held that the policy was not narrowly tailored. It violated the Equal Protection Clause by not providing considering each applicant individually. "The . . . automatic distribution of 20 points has the effect of making 'the factor of race . . . decisive' for virtually every minimally qualified underrepresented minority applicant." It was too much like an automatic preference, just based on the status of the applicant as a minority.

The result was different when the Court turned to the affirmative action policy of Michigan's law school. In *Grutter*, by a 5-4 margin, the

Court held that this policy did not violate the Equal Protection Clause. Thus it was constitutional.

Justice Sandra Day O'Connor wrote for the majority. "Government may treat people differently because of their race only for the most compelling reasons," O'Connor wrote. "Today we endorse [the] view that student body diversity is a compelling state interest that can justify the use of race in university admissions. When race-based action is necessary to further a compelling government interest, such action does not violate the constitutional guarantee of equal protection so long as the narrow-tailoring requirement is also satisfied."

Justice O'Connor said the admissions policy did not create a quota. "Truly individualized consideration demands that race be used in a flexible, nonmechanical way . . . Universities can . . . consider race or ethnicity . . . as a 'plus' factor [when individually considering] each and every applicant."

Four justices dissented. Justice Clarence Thomas was very forceful. "[R]acial classifications are *per se* [in themselves] harmful and . . . almost no amount of benefit in the eye of the beholder can justify such classifications."

IMPACT OF THE DECISIONS

The decisions gave colleges guidelines as to what is permitted and what is not. The decisions were limited to higher education. It is not clear whether they would apply to affirmative action programs in other fields such as getting a job or a government contract.

QUESTIONS

1. Is affirmative action consistent with "equal protection"? Why or why not?

_____

_____

2. *Plessy's* "separate but equal" doctrine put African Americans at a severe disadvantage. *Grutter's* approval of affirmative action gave African Americans and other minorities an advantage in getting into law school. The dissents in both cases argued that the Constitution is color-blind. Is it? Should it be?

_____

_____

Case 24: United States v. American Library Association (2003)
Internet Filters in Libraries

> **THE ISSUE** Does a public library violate the First Amendment by installing Internet filtering software on its public computers?

WHAT'S AT STAKE?

The constitutionality of a federal law called the Children's Internet Protection Act. The law was designed to protect children from being exposed to pornography in public libraries.

FACTS AND BACKGROUND

President Clinton signed the Children's Internet Protection Act (CIPA) into law in 2000. The law says public libraries that accept federal money to help pay for Internet access must install "filtering" software. This is supposed to block any pornographic images from coming through.

A group of library associations sued to block these filtering requirements. They argued that by linking money and filters, the law encouraged public libraries to violate the First Amendment's guarantees of free speech. Everyone agreed that it was OK for libraries to refuse to display pornography (because pornography isn't protected speech under the Constitution). But the library associations and the government disagreed about installing Internet filters. If the filters tended to block some non-pornographic sites along with pornographic ones, would that violate library patrons' First Amendment rights?

The libraries acknowledged that the law allows anyone to ask a librarian to unblock a specific website. It also allows adults to ask that the filter be turned off altogether. But they argued that people using the library would find these remedies embarrassing and impractical.

THE DECISION

In June 2003, the nine justices issued five separate opinions. Six justices voted to uphold the law. However, they could not agree on the reasons for doing so. As a result, the Court issued a "plurality opinion." This is an opinion that announces the Court's decision even though a majority of at least five judges hasn't signed onto that opinion's reasoning. In this case, the plurality opinion was authored by Chief Justice Rehnquist and joined by Justices O'Connor, Scalia and Thomas. Justices Kennedy and Breyer filed their own separate opinions—"concurring" in the plurality's judgment but not its reasoning.

THE PLURALITY OPINION

Justice Rehnquist explained that the law does not require any library to accept federal money. They can do without the money. If they do, they don't have to install Internet filters.

Congress can attach conditions to receiving federal money. Those conditions must not "induce the recipient to engage in activities that would themselves be unconstitutional." However, Rehnquist concluded that Congress did not commit that error in this case. He noted that most libraries already exclude pornography from their print collections. And he didn't think the tendency of filtering software to "overblock" non-pornographic sites was a real constitutional problem. When adult patrons encounter a blocked site, they can ask a librarian to unblock it or have the filter disabled entirely.

THE DISSENTS

Justice Stevens viewed CIPA "as a blunt nationwide restraint on adult access to an enormous amount of valuable" and often constitution-ally protected speech. Justice Souter dissented in an opinion joined by Justice Ginsburg. Souter noted that he would have joined the plurality if the only First Amendment interests raised in this case were those of children rather than those of adults.

IMPACT OF THE DECISION

Prior to CIPA, many parents objected to libraries' Internet terminals making hardcore pornography available to children. Some parents also expressed concern when they learned that some adults were viewing such material on terminals with children nearby. Libraries, on the other hand, were equally determined to defend their patrons' right to conduct efficient and full Web searches. Will the law upheld by the Court in this case withstand the test of time? That may depend on whether filtering technology continues to improve. It may also hinge on whether library patrons are able to have erroneously blocked sites easily unblocked.

QUESTION

1. Do you think that Internet Filters in public libraries violate the First Amendment? Explain your answer.

_____

_____

Case 25:
Terrorism Cases (2004)   Due Process Rights in Wartime

THE ISSUES These two cases asked
1. Can the government hold American citizens for a long, open-ended period as "enemy combatants" and not permit them to ask American courts whether they are held legally?
2. Do foreigners captured overseas and jailed at Guantanamo Bay, Cuba, have the right to ask American courts to decide whether they are being held legally?

WHAT'S AT STAKE?

The balance between the government's powers to fight terrorism and the Constitution's promise of due process.

FACTS AND BACKGROUND
Detaining American Citizens

The man at the heart of *Hamdi* v. *Rumsfeld* was Yaser Esam Hamdi. He was captured in Afghanistan in late 2001.

The U.S. military said Hamdi was an enemy combatant, "engaged in an armed conflict against the United States." Later, the military learned that Hamdi had been born in Louisiana. That made him a United States citizen, even though he'd lived almost all his life in other countries.

Hamdi's attorney said that Hamdi deserved the due process rights that other Americans have. He should have a hearing in court so he could argue that he never was an enemy combatant. The attorney said, "we have never authorized *detention* [jailing] of a citizen in this country without giving him an opportunity to be heard, to say, hey, I am an innocent person."

The government replied "it has the authority to hold . . . enemy combatants captured on the battlefield . . . to prevent them from returning to the battle."

Detaining Foreigners at Guantanamo Bay

The prisoners in *Rasul* v. *Bush* also claimed they were wrongly imprisoned. They wanted a court hearing. But do United States courts have jurisdiction to consider challenges from foreigners captured abroad and jailed at the Guantanamo Bay Naval Base in Cuba?

The government was holding about 650 foreigners at Guantanamo Bay. The government said they were al Qaeda fighters.

Guantanamo Bay Naval Base is on Cuban soil. But Cuba leases the base to the U.S. The U.S. military has used it for over 100 years. In a previous case, the Court had ruled, "if an alien [foreigner] is outside the country's sovereign territory, then . . . the alien is not permitted access to the courts of the United States to enforce the Constitution."

THE DECISIONS

In *Hamdi*, the Court ruled 6-3 that Hamdi had a right to a hearing. Justice Sandra Day O'Connor wrote the Court's opinion. She said the Court has "made clear that a state of war is not a blank check for the president when it comes to the rights of the nation's citizens." She added, "history and common sense teach us that an unchecked system of detention [can lead to] oppression and abuse."

   Rasul was also decided by a 6-3 margin. Justice John Paul Stevens wrote for the Court. He noted that the prisoners have been held for more than two years in territory that the United States controls. Thus, even though they are not on U.S. soil, they can ask U. S. courts if their detention is legal.

THE IMPACT OF THE DECISIONS

The government decided not to prosecute Hamdi. It let him leave the country, on the condition that he renounce his U.S. citizenship and agree not to travel to certain countries. The cases of the foreign nationals challenging their detention as enemy combatants had not been finally determined when this book went to press.

QUESTIONS

1. What did the Court hold in *Hamdi*? Why? Do you agree?

_____

_____

2. What did the Court hold in *Rasul*? Why? Do you agree?

_____

_____

FIND OUT

Did the United States ever before detain American citizens without giving them access to the courts? Did the Japanese-Americans detained in World War II have access to the courts?

ONLINE EXTRA

Read the online case of *Ex Parte Milligan*. Did the prisoners in that case have a right to go to court? Why or why not?

More Information About the Supreme Court

Websites

The Administrative Office of the U. S. Courts has a useful introduction to the Supreme Court:
http://www.uscourts.gov/

The U. S. Supreme Court's own site also contains a good introduction:
http://www.supremecourtus.gov/

The Supreme Court Historical Society contains information about a number of landmark cases, including some involving students: http://www.supremecourthistory.org

The Landmark Cases site looks at many key Supreme Court cases, including a number covered in this book: http://www.landmarkcases.org

The Bill of Rights Institute contains a wealth of material on cases dealing with the first ten amendments to the U. S. Constitution:
http://www.billofrightsinstitute.org

The First Amendment Center naturally focuses on the many cases that raise issues under than amendment This link will take you to the part of the site that focuses on the First Amendment in schools. http://www.firstamendmentschools.org

The Minnesota Center for Community Legal Education has good information on understanding the federal court system and some landmark cases: http://www.civicallyspeaking.org

The About.com site has information about the Supreme Court and its procedures:
http://usgovinfo.about.com/blcthistory.htm

The Pagewise site has a very brief introduction to the Court:
http://mnmn.essortment.com/supremecourthi_rljv.htm

Books

For a good introduction to the Court, at the appropriate reading level, see John J. Patrick's *Supreme Court of the United States: A Student Companion* (Oxford Student Companions to American Government). For more on the Constitution, see Syl Sobel and Denise Gilgannon's *The U.S. Constitution and You*.

There are a number of biographies of Supreme Court justices for young people. Enslow publishes a series that includes biographies of such justices as John Marshall, Roger Tawney, Earl Warren, Thurgood Marshall, and Sandra Day O'Connor.

Lisa Aldred's biography of Thurgood Marshall in the Black Americans of Achievement series is written for young adults. Other young adult biographies of Marshall are Joe Arthur's *The Story of Thurgood Marshall: Justice for All*, Carla Williams' *Thurgood Marshall (Journey to Freedom)*, and Geoffrey M. Horn's *Thurgood Marshall* (Trailblazers of the Modern World).

Sandra Day O'Connor has also been the subject of biographies for young people. See by Jean Kinney Williams, *Sandra Day O'Connor: Lawyer and Supreme Court Justice* (Ferguson Career Biographies) and two books by Lisa Tucker McElroy, *Meet My Grandmother: She's a Supreme Court Justice* and *Sandra Day O'Connor: Supreme Court Justice*.

For a biography of John Marshall for young people, see Francis X. Stites, *John Marshall: Defender of the Constitution*.

For a young adult biography of Earl Warren, see Christine L. Compston, *Earl Warren: Justice for All* (Oxford Portraits).

Supreme Court Cases

A young adult biography in the same series looks at an eloquent justice who served in the early days of the last century. See G. Edward White's *Oliver Wendell Holmes: Sage of the Supreme Court* (Oxford Portraits).

A

acquit find not guilty after a criminal trial

admissible evidence that can be legally and properly introduced in a civil or criminal trial

affirmed ruling by the Supreme Court or another appeals court that the lower court's decision or order is valid and will stand

amicus curiae Latin term meaning "friend of the court"; party who volunteers information on some aspect of a case or law to assist the court in its deliberation; An **amicus brief** is a document filed by an amicus curiae in support of a party in a lawsuit.

appeal request by the losing party in a lawsuit that a higher court review the judgment

appellant party who begins an appeal; Sometimes called a petitioner

appellate court court having **jurisdiction** [authority] to hear appeals and review a **trial court**'s procedure; The Supreme Court is an appellate court.

appellee party against whom an appeal is taken; sometimes called a respondent

at issue the points or opposite positions in dispute or under consideration in a lawsuit

B

brief written statement prepared by one side in a lawsuit to explain to the court its view of the facts of a case and the law governing the case

burden of proof duty of proving the facts in dispute in a lawsuit; The burden is on the **prosecutor**—the person pursuing a criminal charge—in a criminal case. It is on the plaintiff—the person bringing the suit—in a civil case.

C

case law law based on published judicial decisions, such as those of the Supreme Court; Law made by the legislature is **statutory law**.

certiorari Latin term meaning "to be informed of"; A **writ** of certiorari is a request to a higher court to review a case. Most Supreme Court cases begin with the Court receiving such a writ.

concurring opinion Supreme Court or other appellate court opinion by one or more judges that agrees with part but not all of the majority opinion in the case

counsel lawyers in a case; also legal advice

court of last resort final court that decides a case on appeal (for example, the Supreme Court of the United States or the supreme court of a state)

custody (criminal law) imprisonment or confinement; A person is in custody when he is detained by police and does not feel that he is free to leave. An arrest puts someone in custody, but so may questioning by police in other settings. Custody is important in criminal law because the police must give a **Miranda warning** to anyone they are questioning in custody. This is called custodial questioning.

D

decision judgment reached or given by a court of law

defendant person being sued (civil case); person accused of committing a crime (criminal case)

dissenting opinion Supreme Court or other appellate court opinion setting forth the minority view and outlining the disagreement of one or more judges with the decision of the majority

U.S. Supreme Court Case Studies

due process clause section of the 14th Amendment specifying that no state shall "deprive any person of life, liberty, and property, without due process of law"

due process of law right of all persons to receive the guarantees and safeguards of the law and the judicial process; Due process includes such constitutional requirements as adequate notice, assistance of **counsel**, and the rights to remain silent, to a speedy and public trial, to an impartial jury, and to confront witnesses.

E

equal protection clause section of the 14th Amendment specifying that no state shall "deny to any person the equal protection of the law"

equal protection of the law guarantee of the 14th Amendment of the U.S. Constitution that all persons receive equal treatment under law

error mistake of law in a judgment or order of a court or in some procedural step in legal proceedings

establishment clause part of the First Amendment that says that "Congress shall make no law respecting an establishment of religion"; This clause prevents the government from sponsoring a particular religion.

exclusionary rule rule preventing evidence obtained illegally from being used in any trial

ex parte on behalf of only one party, without notice to any other party; For example, a request for a search warrant is an ex parte proceeding, since the person subject to the search is not notified of the proceeding and is not present during the hearing. An **ex parte proceeding** is one in which only one side is represented.

F

free exercise clause section of the First Amendment that says that Congress shall make no law "prohibiting the free exercise of religion"; This clause prevents the government from denying anyone the freedom to worship.

H

habeas corpus Latin phrase meaning "you have the body"; A **writ** [court order] that commands that a person be brought before a judge. Most commonly, a writ of habeas corpus is a legal document that forces law enforcement authorities to produce a prisoner they are holding and to legally justify his or her detention.

I

injunction order of the court prohibiting (or compelling) the performance of a specific act to prevent damage or injury that cannot be repaired

J

judicial review courts' review of the official actions of other branches of government; the authority to declare the actions of other branches **unconstitutional**

jurisdiction power, right, or authority to apply the law; a court's authority to decide a case; also, the territory from which a court is authorized to hear cases

jury certain number of persons selected according to law and sworn to inquire into matters of fact and declare the truth about matters of fact before them; A trial jury is usually composed of six to twelve persons and can hear either civil or criminal cases.

M

Miranda warning requirement that police tell a suspect in their **custody** of his/her constitutional rights before they question him/her; named as a result of the Supreme Court's *Miranda* v. *Arizona* ruling establishing such requirements

O

opinion written decision of the Supreme Court or another appellate court

oral argument portion of a Supreme Court or other appellate case in which the lawyers appear before the court to summarize their position and also to answer questions from the justices

order written or oral command from a court directing or forbidding an action

overrule decision by higher court finding that a lower court decision was in error

P

plurality opinion decision of a court when a majority agrees with the decision but not with the reasoning

precedent previously decided case that guides future decisions

prior restraint taking legal action before an anticipated wrongdoing; form of censorship in which government officials (attempt to) restrict a newspaper, magazine, or other publication in advance from publishing materials of which they disapprove

prosecutor government lawyer, such as a district attorney, who tries criminal cases

public defender lawyer employed by the government to represent individuals accused of crimes who cannot afford to hire their own lawyer privately

pure speech speech using words; compare with **symbolic speech**

R

remand send a dispute back to the court where it was originally heard; Remand often happens when an appellate court sends a case back to a lower court for further proceedings.

reverse action of a higher court in setting aside or revoking a lower court decision because of an error; A reversal is often accompanied by a **remand** to the lower court that heard the case.

reversible error mistake of law sufficiently harmful to justify reversing the judgment of a lower court

S

search warrant written order issued by a judge that directs a law enforcement officer to search a specific area for a specific piece of evidence

self-incrimination, privilege against constitutional right of a person to refuse to give testimony against himself or herself if that testimony could subject him or her to criminal prosecution; found in the Fifth Amendment; often referred to as "taking the Fifth"

standing legal right to bring a lawsuit; Only a person with something at stake has standing to bring a lawsuit.

stare decisis Latin term meaning "to stand by that which was decided"; When a court has once laid down a principle of law as applicable to a certain set of facts, it will adhere to that principle and apply it to future cases where the facts are substantially the same.

statute law enacted by legislatures or executive officers

U.S. Supreme Court Case Studies

strike down a law make a law invalid or void, as if it had never existed; happens when a court finds a law unconstitutional

symbolic speech actions that try to persuade without words; examples would be wearing armbands or political buttons

T

temporary restraining order (TRO) court order prohibiting a person from an action that is likely to cause harm that can't be repaired; A TRO differs from an **injunction** in that it may be granted immediately, without notice to the opposing party and without a hearing. A TRO lasts only until a hearing can be held.

trial court court that first hears a case and determines issues of fact and law; Appellate courts such as the Supreme Court review the work of trial courts.

U

unconstitutional conflicting with some provision of a constitution; A law found to be unconstitutional is considered **void**.

V

void of no force or legal effect

W

ward person who is under the control of a guardian or under the protection of the court because of an incapacity, such as being a minor

writ court order directing a person to do (or not do) something

U.S. Supreme Court Case Studies